He's Just My Dad!

JUNIOR SEAU'S SON, JAKE

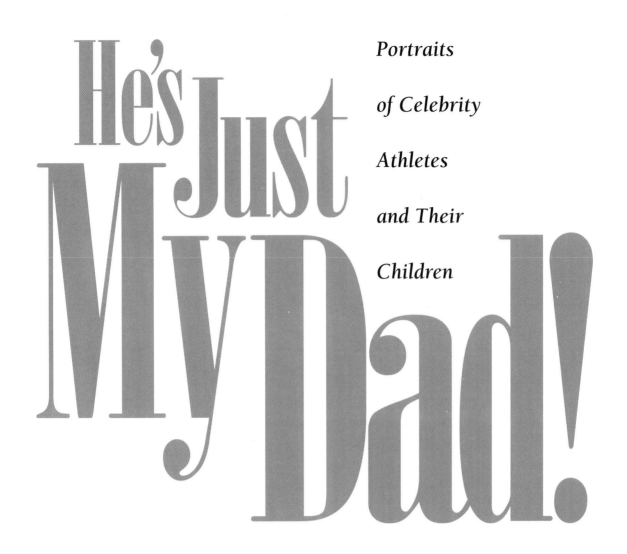

He's Just My Dad!

Portraits of Celebrity Athletes and Their Children

DIANE LONG

FOREWORD BY JOHN GRISHAM
AFTERWORD BY DAVID ROBINSON

HarperEntertainment
An Imprint of HarperCollinsPublishers

Permissions and acknowledgments appear on pages 163-64.

The author wishes to acknowledge the Ford Motor Company and Value America for their generous support of this project. Proceeds from the sale of this book will benefit the Boys and Girls Clubs and CASA—Court Appointed Special Advocates.

HE'S JUST MY DAD! PORTRAITS OF CELEBRITY ATHLETES AND THEIR CHILDREN.
Text copyright © 2000 by Diane Long.
Introduction copyright © 2000 by Diane Long.
Foreword copyright © 2000 by John Grisham.
Afterword copyright © 2000 by David Robinson.

HarperCollins books may be purchased for educational, business, or sales promotional use. For information, please write to Special Markets Department, HarperCollins Publishers Inc., 10 East 53rd Street, New York, N.Y. 10022.

FIRST EDITION

Designed by Gibson Design Associates
Produced by Merry and Frank Thomasson in association with Diane Long

Printed on acid-free paper

Library of Congress Cataloging-in-Publication Data has been applied for.

ISBN 0-06-105148-9

00 01 02 03 04   10 9 8 7 6 5 4 3 2 1

For the two most important dads in my life.
To my father, Frank, whose love, optimism, and values will
always inspire me. To my husband, Howie, for sharing my
dreams and filling my heart. I love them both tremendously
and thank them for the gifts they have given our sons.

DIANE

Contents

Foreword • John Grisham   viii

Introduction   x

Terry Bradshaw • Rachel & Erin   1

Roger Clemens • Koby, Kory, Kacy & Kody   6

Governor Jesse Ventura • Jade & Tyrel   10

Ronnie Lott • Hailey, Isaiah & Chloe   15

Isiah Thomas • Joshua & Lauren   18

Yogi Berra • Larry, Tim & Dale   23

Sinjin Smith • Hagen & Stanton   27

Dan Marino • Daniel, Michael, Joey, Ali & Niki   30

Ivan "Pudge" Rodriguez • Derrick & Amanda   37

Brett Favre • Brittany & Breleigh   40

Scott Stevens • Kaitlin, Ryan & Kara   44

Dan Jansen • Jane & Olivia   49

Gary Gait • Braden & Taylor   52

Tom Kite • Stephanie, Paul & David   55

Terry Porter • Brianna, Franklin & Malcom   58

Tino Martinez • Olivia, TJ & Victoria   62

Dominik Hasek • Michael & Dominika   66

Tony Meola • Jonathan   69

Junior Seau • Sydney & Jake   73

Richard Petty • Kyle, Sharon, Lisa & Rebecca   78

Kyle Petty • Adam, Austin & Montgomery Lee   83

Michael Weiss • Annie Mae   87

Greg LeMond • Geoffrey, Scott & Simone   90

Bill Walton • Luke, Nathan, Adam & Chris   92

Scott Tinley • Torrie & Dane   99

Reggie White • Jeremy & Jocolia   102

Keith Van Horn • Sabrina & Nicholas   108

Howie Long • Chris, Kyle & Howie   112

Orel Hershiser • Quinton & Jordan   118

Peter Vidmar • Timothy, Christopher, Stephen, Kathryn & Emily   123

John Starks • John Jr. & Chelsea   126

Shane Sellers • Shali, Saban & Steiner   131

Doug Flutie • Alexa & Dougie   135

Wayne Gretzky • Pauline, Ty & Trevor   139

Joe Montana • Alexandra, Elizabeth, Nathanial & Nicholas   145

Peter Vermes • Nicole & Kyle   148

John Elway • Jessica, Jack, Jordan & Juliana   155

Afterword • David Robinson   161

Foreword

by John Grisham

TWENTY-FIVE YEARS AGO I DECIDED NOT to become a professional athlete. I didn't want to put pressure on my kids.

Of course I didn't have any kids back then, and, to be perfectly honest, I didn't exactly walk away from a lucrative contract, nor a nonlucrative one.

Too short for basketball, too slow for football, but just perfect for baseball, or so I thought. Hey, first team all-conference in high school. What can I say? Like all the kids in my neighborhood, I grew up with the dream of baseball immortality. It wasn't a question of making it to the major leagues, we were more concerned with which team we would play for. I secretly worried about making it to the Hall of Fame.

To my surprise, my name was not mentioned in the June 1973 amateur draft. Undaunted, I walked on at a nearby junior college, made the team, and one day when I was nineteen I stood in the batter's box and watched in horror as a 90 m.p.h. fastball came in my general direction. I could hardly see it; it looked like an aspirin. I certainly wanted no part of it. Since it had already been determined that I could not hit a curveball, there wasn't much left. Pitchers can be cruel when they spot weaknesses.

But dreams of glory die slowly, and I was not ready to admit that I might not make it to the Bigs. I hung around the game for a couple of years, telling myself some keen-eyed scout, someone with real vision, would notice the talent that everyone else had missed. This scout was never heard from. In fact, there may have been more than one of them, but we'll never know. I finally hung up my spikes and headed for law school.

As the years have passed, I have slowly realized how far-fetched my dreams were. I was a decent athlete in high school, but not nearly good enough for the college game. And to play professionally—I must have been hallucinating.

Professional athletes are aberrations; they're not like the rest of us. They are blessed with genes that give them speed and agility and size and toughness. They have a burning desire to work, to train, to endure beyond a point where most others quit. Most get a lucky break or two, but they also create their own luck.

As a culture we admire and emulate and even idolize them. They become famous and get paid large sums of money for playing the games we loved as children. They endorse shoes and cars and Wheaties and get mobbed outside of ballparks. Their problems become headlines. Their victories are celebrated by millions.

They are stars who are larger than life, heroes who are lucky enough to live the dreams of our youth. Their lives are fairy tales.

But are they really that different?

The athletes in the pages that follow are instantly recognizable. We know them by their first names. We've watched their careers, memorized their stats, bought expensive tickets so we could see them play. We've cheered them and booed them, and deep down inside we've secretly wished that we could be them.

But as gifted and as famous as they might be, they honor a more important calling. Off the field and away from the crowds, they are simply dads, devoted fathers with their priorities in order. They are there at birth, at baptism, at preschool, at the recitals, at the first T-ball game and the last prom. They cheer from the bleachers and cry when their little one's hurt. They share the laughs and the losses. They read bedtime stories, help with homework, and dispense fatherly advice. They take refuge from the strains of celebrityhood by doing what other dads do—they go play with their kids. They have learned, some no doubt the hard way, that careers are temporary but kids are forever.

Look at the faces of their children, and you will not see the concerns of "Did you win?" or "Did you lose?" or "Can you make the playoffs?" The fathers may be famous, but the children are not particularly impressed by it. They want their fathers at home to listen, to help, to love, to play. And their fathers are there, doing the same things that all good dads do.

Ask any one of these kids if their father is a famous athlete, and you're likely to hear, "No, he's just my dad."

Introduction

PEOPLE ASK ME WHY I DECIDED TO PUT this book together. Watching our boys and the way they interact with their dad has shown me very clearly how enormously important their dad is to them. How a cuddle on the couch can dry tears of fear or anxiety or hurt. How a ride to the store with dad for some frozen yogurt can help take the sting out of a classmate's harsh words. How a dad's humor can diffuse a rant about the inequities of being the middle child.

For years I have watched Howie and our boys just being together. And those are the moments I treasure. But more than that, I know those are the moments Howie treasures—and in that small revelation, the true essence of a dad is revealed.

My husband, Howie, is one of the greatest fathers in the world, plain and simple. That's a fact. It is also true that he was not always an exemplary dad.

HOWIE LONG AND CHRIS

Fifteen years ago when our first son, Christopher, was born, Howie was a young man from a small college obsessively fighting for credibility in the National Football League. He was intense and single-minded. All of his time was spent either training his body or his mind to be the best football player he could. Each week he worked with a fervent drive to surpass his performance the week before. To him, his efforts were never good enough. He felt constant pressure to live up to his contract terms and prove himself in the league. With so much of his attention focused on his professional life, his energies were not geared toward what it took to be a father.

Howie didn't have the slightest idea of what to do, so he loved Christopher as much as humanly possible and supported me in what I decided to do with him. All of the primary parenting duties fell on me. Sure, he would often pick up the golden-haired baby and toss him in the air, causing contagious laughter. But I can't recall all that many times that he changed diapers or initiated one-on-one excursions.

Then something happened as our family grew with the birth of Kyle and young Howie. Maybe it was maturity, maybe it was acquired knowledge, life experience, concentrated association with other parents, or the realization that what is truly important eclipses career successes. Gradually, Howie began to choose to spend time with the boys—together and individually. It wasn't just out of obligation, but the sheer enjoyment and bliss he experienced from being with his sons. He sought out and created opportunities where he could take the boys to school or to the movies, to play catch, or read a book.

It was about five years ago when I suddenly realized that Howie had become an emotionally present parent. I remember being zapped with a feeling of overwhelming joy. Not only was Howie spending time, energy, patience, and passion in his fathering, he was loving every minute of it. He had clearly chosen fatherhood over everything else.

I began to notice that a majority of the well-known men in the world of athletics with whom I came in contact lead very family-oriented, very normal, very grounded lives at home. Their work hours are different than those of most, and travel is the norm. But having practiced law, I know that people in all occupations must balance hours spent with their families against career obligations. Regardless of their personal parenting styles, among most of the icons of the athletic world, one thing was very clear: their families were their first priority.

That is as it should be. We all know that there is no press coverage or award for putting your family first. But in a world where we are bombarded with negative headlines about athletes who are anything but heroes, and stories about deadbeat dads who make babies without ever intending to act as fathers, I got to thinking that rarely does anyone make a big fuss about the good guys.

He's Just My Dad! is a fuss about the good guys. This project is intended to encourage and uplift families. It is my hope that these photos will inspire all parents to strive to be superstars with their own children by savoring the opportunities for special moments in the most ordinary circumstances. It is in these everyday experiences that real beauty manifests itself when a dad sees and communicates with his child's soul by saying, "I know exactly who you are and I love you and want to be loved by you."

I should stress that this book is by no means intended to be an all-star team of greatest dads. It is simply a compilation of a representative group of men who have made a commitment to real fatherhood and to their children. The group of families included was defined by the practical limitations of family and school schedules, team schedules and seasons, and daylight. Nevertheless, the group makes quite an impressive team.

The heart of this book is the children. In the well-loved book *The Little Prince*, it is said "only the children know what they are looking for." The children were my guides for this book. I was astonished by how cooperative each and every child was during the photographic and interview processes. They contributed ideas for how and where the photos should be taken and participated in interviewing their fathers. They were smart, funny, curious, outgoing, and candid. Without the children and the guidance of their hearts, this book would not have been possible.

The celebrity athletes featured in *He's Just My Dad!* are great sports for being a part of this book. They generously opened up their homes and personal space to provide us with these delicious unstaged glimpses. They discussed their personal styles of guiding, teaching, and interacting with their children. They were open, cooperative, gracious, easygoing, and just plain nice. They responded to the children's direction with a blended sense of duty and humor.

During the time I spent with these celebrity athletes, I learned several things: They smile when asked about their career accomplishments, but beam when they discuss their children. They speak softly, act gently, are proud of their families, have surprisingly kid-oriented yards (lots of primary-colored plastic), acknowledge that they were fortunate to be professional athletes, worry about their children learning to deal with disappointment and other realities of life, and easily melt when they hear the words "Pleeeeease Daddy." I learned that there are real heroes in America. They are found in the car pool lines, in the backyards, at the homework tables, and wherever hugs, encouragement, and support are needed—they are dads.

What I love about Howie is not that he was a dynamic defensive lineman or that he is a sharp and engaging football broadcaster, but that he is an incredible father to our three sons. I thought it would be fascinating to reveal the same sweet secret about other celebrity athletes—and so *He's Just My Dad!* was born.

Diane Fay

Terry Bradshaw
Rachel & Erin

We were in California and he was awarded the best, I don't know, pro football caster of the year or something, and instead of him doing the interviews, he let us say things and be in every picture. He made it really special for us, too.

—RACHEL

**HOW ARE YOUR
PERSONALITIES
MOST ALIKE?**
Erin: *Shy. Shy.*
Rachel: *I'm not shy!*
Erin: *I'm shy!*
Terry: *We can all be*
LOUDMOUTHS! *We're
very theatrical, and
creative . . . we talk
with our hands a lot.
The only difference
is that the girls are
extremely intelligent.*

Terry Bradshaw, a native of Shreveport, Louisiana, was born September 2, 1948, and became one of the most outstanding quarterbacks in NFL History. As a member of the Pittsburgh Steelers, he led his team to four Super Bowl championships in six seasons, winning MVP of the Super Bowl in both 1979 and 1980. Bradshaw was the regular season MVP in 1978, and was elected to Pro Football's Hall of Fame in 1989, his first year of eligibility. He was the first player chosen in the 1970 draft, and led the previously troubled Steelers franchise to six AFC title games during that decade. After retiring prior to the 1984 season, Bradshaw embarked on a broadcasting career with CBS Sports (1984–1993) and FOX (1994–present). Bradshaw has bankrolled his avuncular country boy image as a widely sought motivational speaker. He's also written three books, launched a recording career, and appeared in several films, including *Cannonball Run. The Sporting News* ranking of the top 100 players of all time listed Bradshaw at number 44.

I love that my daughters took such a great interest in horses. They started riding when they were five and three. Erin kept falling asleep and falling off. Then they wanted to compete. It made me nervous at first. Not nervous because I was hoping they would win, but nervous hoping that they understood that when they don't win it's okay.

—TERRY

Roger Clemens
Koby, Kory, Kacy & Kody

*I think people would be
surprised that my dad is
a really good bowler.*

—KOBY

*When I play baseball I like to
make my tough face.*
                    —KODY

Roger Clemens, born August 4, 1962, is one of the finest pitchers in Major League Baseball history. He is the only pitcher to win five Cy Young Awards (1986, 1987, 1991, 1997, 1998). He led the American League in earned run average in six different seasons. Only Lefty Grove (nine times) ever led more. His 3,316 strikeouts (through the 1999 season) ranks ninth on the all-time list. Only Nolan Ryan, Randy Johnson, and Sandy Koufax have more career games with 10 or more strikeouts. Clemens shares the major league record for strikeouts in a game (20, which he did twice). He was the American League MVP and Cy Young Award winner in the same season (1986). He is a seven-time all-star, and was elected by the fans as one of the six pitchers on the All Century Team. On October 27, 1999, Clemens pitched and won the deciding game of the World Series, becoming a World Champion for the first time. Unlike most of the other great pitchers in history, Clemens pitched his entire career in the American League pitching to designated hitters. And he spent the first 13 seasons of his career in Boston's Fenway Park, known as a hitter's paradise. The future Hall of Famer has won 20 or more games in five different seasons.

It's hard with four boys to make sure they all get the individual attention they need. It works because I just love being their dad.

—Roger

I like to wrestle with my dad.
I always win, even though he
tries to cheat.

—KACY

Governor Jesse Ventura
Jade & Tyrel

Listen to them and pay attention . . .
REALLY pay attention because
maybe what YOU think isn't important.
What THEY think is!

—JESSE

He's a BIG teddy bear to us.

—JADE

Jesse Ventura's victory when elected Governor of Minnesota represents a major political upset. Born July 15, 1951, Jesse is a former U.S. Navy SEAL, a former professional wrestler, a Hollywood film actor, a broadcaster for radio and TV, and author, in addition to being governor. After he was honorably discharged from the Navy, he started his career as Jesse "The Body" Ventura. Jesse was a great wrestler. With Adrian Adonis, he won the tag team title. At one time, he had a big feud with Hulk Hogan. The WWF hired Ventura to do a talk show following the 1980s legend Rowdy Roddy Piper's show; Jesse's show was called *The Body Shop*. In 1987, Ventura's wrestling career ended. The official reason: he had been exposed to Agent Orange in Vietnam and due to health reasons could not wrestle anymore. Ventura became the first Reform Party candidate elected to governor. As a politician, he has been as outrageous and unpredictable as he was when wrestling. On why he favors gay and lesbian rights, he said, "Love is bigger than government." In an interview given to television reporters just before he went hunting, he quipped, "We're going to give the press a ten minute head start, and that's what we're going to hunt." Ventura published *I Ain't Got Time to Bleed: Reworking the Body Politic from the Bottom Up*. The book takes its title from the best-remembered line in Ventura's film debut, *Predator*.

Dad taught me to stick to my goals, never change my personality, always stay who I am.

—Tyrel

The boys in my class say, "I saw your dad on TV last night." I never watch my dad on TV. I don't really like football, it's BORING! Plus, I get to see him all the time.

—HAILEY

Ronnie Lott
Hailey, Isaiah & Chloe

*Daddy tucks me in for bed
and gives me hugs and kisses.*

—CHLOE

When I'm hanging out with my dad, we play Legos. But he's not very good at Legos . . . he doesn't put them in the right places.

—ISAIAH

Ronnie Lott, born May 8, 1959, was one of the most remarkable players in NFL history. According to a 1999 *Sporting News* list of the 100 top players, Lott is 23rd best of all time, and the top defensive back ever. A member of four Super Bowl championship teams with the San Francisco 49ers, Lott played in 10 Pro Bowls and intercepted 63 passes while recording more than 1,000 crushing tackles. He was a first round pick in 1981, and went on to enjoy a rookie season that saw him reach All-Pro honors and the Super Bowl. His greatest season may have been 1984, when the 49ers went 15–1 (losing only to the Steelers by three points) and went on to beat Miami in the Super Bowl. That season the entire 49ers' secondary (Lott, Eric Wright, Carlton Williamson, and Dwight Hicks) went to the Pro Bowl. After ten seasons in San Francisco, Lott signed with the Los Angeles Raiders for two years, and finished his career playing with the New York Jets for two seasons. He retired in 1994 and was inducted into the Pro Football Hall of Fame in 2000. After his playing career, Lott went into broadcasting with FOX Sports as both a studio and game analyst. Famed coach Bill Parcells always claimed that of all the great athletes he coached against, Lott was the one he admired most as a player.

Isiah Thomas, born April 30, 1961, was one of the most brilliant players in the history of the NBA. Before his spectacular 13-year career with the Detroit Pistons, Thomas grew up the youngest of nine children in West Chicago. He became a member of two NBA Championship teams, participated in 11 All-Star Games (twice being named MVP), and was selected as one of the 50 greatest players for the 1996 NBA 50th Anniversary All Time Team. He was MVP of the 1990 NBA Finals, and his clutch performances are legendary. In game six of the 1988 Finals, he scored a record 25 points in one quarter versus the Los Angeles Lakers. Nicknamed "Zeke," he was selected to play for the United States in the 1980 Olympic Games. The U.S. boycott ruined his chance for a gold medal. But in 1981, Thomas led Bob Knight's Indiana Hoosiers to the NCAA Championship. He left after his sophomore season for the Pistons, but fulfilled a promise to his mother by gradua-ting six years later with a degree in criminal justice. Isiah served as president of the Players Association, and after retirement he became part owner of the Toronto Raptors. After leaving Toronto, Thomas entered broadcasting, and in 1997, bought the CBA, hoping to build up the minor leagues of professional basketball.

Isiah Thomas
Joshua & Lauren

He's a great dad because he plays football with me and sometimes he lets me win.

—LAUREN

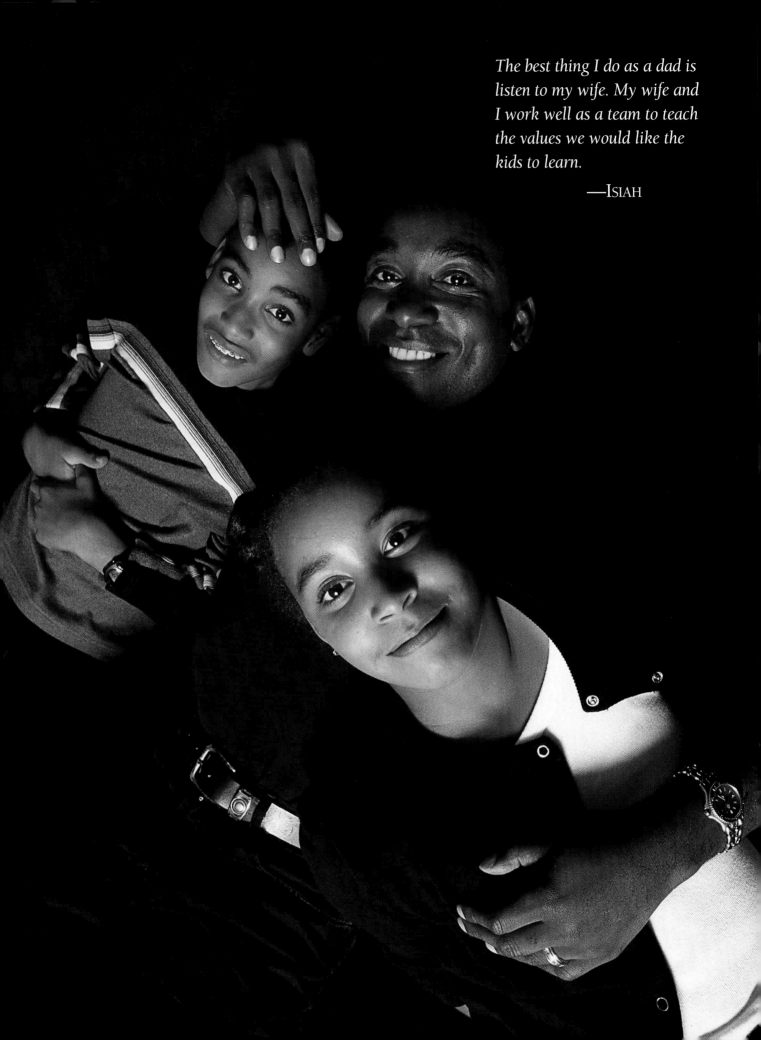

The best thing I do as a dad is listen to my wife. My wife and I work well as a team to teach the values we would like the kids to learn.

—ISIAH

TALKING ABOUT GIRLS . . .

Isiah: *Does she know you like her?*

Joshua: *Duh!*

Lauren: *He's not one of these nerdy kids who keeps it a secret and plays hard to get.*

Joshua: *Will somebody clue Daddy in on this girl thing! No, she asked me to carry some bags for her. Then I asked her, "Do you want to go to the dance?"*

Isiah: *And what did she say?*

Joshua: *YEA! Now, when you pick me up from the dance—you've got to pick me up in the nice car. And wear that hat.*

Isiah: *What? The chauffeur hat? I don't think so.*

Yogi Berra
Larry, Tim & Dale

You know when I used to be a pain in the neck to them? When I came home from playing ball and they'd want to play catch, I'd say, "Get out of here, you've got brothers you can play catch with!"

—YOGI

*When we were growing up
people in the neighborhood
didn't expect us to be especially great athletes. We
were lucky that way.
Sometimes in high school
kids on the opposing teams
would find out who our dad
was and then we just had
to do our thing and not
worry about it. It was easy
growing up.*

—TIM

Lawrence Peter "Yogi" Berra, born May 12, 1925, in a St. Louis, Missouri, neighborhood known as "The Hill," was one of the most famous baseball players of all time. He was elected to the Hall of Fame in 1972, and was voted onto the All Century Team in 1999 as one of the two best catchers ever. For a seven-year period, he was one of the four best players in baseball at any position, judging by the MVP voting. Beginning in 1950, Berra placed in the top four of the MVP voting (winning three times) from 1950–1956. Berra led the American League in home runs over a ten-year period, and played in 15 All-Star Games. He set numerous World Series records that stand to this day. He hit a home run in the 1950 Series clincher, hit two homers in Game Seven of the 1956 series, and caught Don Larsen's perfect game. As a manager, he led the Yankees to the 1964 pennant, and the Mets to the 1973 pennant. He is at least as famous for his popular sayings, such as "It's déjà vu all over again"; "It gets late early out there"; "No one goes there anymore, it's too popular," and is included in *Bartlett's Quotations*. In early 1999, Berra opened the Yogi Berra Museum in Montclair, New Jersey. It is host to a minor league ballpark and extensive exhibits that chronicle his career.

We used to wrestle with him all the time, but then it got to the point where we were able to overpower him, and he'd start biting and pinching. He said, "What, do you think I'm going to let you beat me?"

—LARRY

Sinjin Smith
Hagen & Stanton

The downside to what I do is the travel. The thing that keeps me going when I'm on the road is knowing that as soon as I walk off the plane I will see their smiling faces.

—SINJIN

Sinjin Smith was born on May 7, 1957. A professional beach volleyball player since 1977, Christopher St. John Smith is one of the most successful players in the history of the sport. He led UCLA to two national championships (1978, 1979) and his college jersey, #22, was retired in 1992 at UCLA's Pauley Pavilion. He was a member of the U.S. National Team from 1979 to 1982. In 1987, he broke Ron Von Hagen's record for career victories, and held the title of world's most prolific player until Karch Kiraly passed him. After partnering with Randy Stokles for most of his career, Smith united with Carl Henkel in 1995 in preparation for the 1996 Olympics in Atlanta, where beach volleyball made its inaugural appearance on the Olympic program. Smith made his Olympic debut in Atlanta, 16 years after being a member of the U.S. indoor volleyball team that missed the boycotted Moscow games. Following the 1996 Olympics (where they finished fifth), Smith and Henkel remained together for the 1997 season. They split for 1998— before rejoining in 1999. From 1998 to 1999, they placed in the top 10 at 21 FIVB beach tour events, finishing second three times. Sinjin's impact on beach volleyball goes beyond wins and losses—he was the first player to get full sponsorship and the first player to secure hats and visors as promotional tools.

When my dad tucks me in, we say a prayer together.

—HAGEN

It is the same prayer my mother taught me when I was a kid. My mom was very happy when she heard Hagen saying that little prayer at bedtime.

—SINJIN

Dan Marino

Daniel, Michael, Joey, Ali & Niki

You adjust as you go. I think I enjoy the time I spend with them a lot more than I did years ago when I didn't think about or appreciate it that much.

—DAN

The trampoline? Sometimes he can't do it.
He broke the trampoline once.

—JOEY

Dan Marino, born September 15, 1961, in Pittsburgh, Pennsylvania, is one of the greatest quarterbacks in NFL history. He was selected by the Miami Dolphins as the 27th pick in the 1983 draft, and quarterbacked the team the next 17-plus years. He is one of only two quarterbacks to have thrown more than 39 touchdown passes in a single season. Marino is also the only man to throw for more than 5,000 yards in a season and the only one with more than 60,000 yards in a career. In 1995, Marino broke Fran Tarkenton's long-standing record for career touchdown passes (342). Marino's total of 414 and counting will stand for years to come. Marino has always been known for his quick release, and his ability to get rid of the ball resulted in the Dolphins consistently being the team that allowed the fewest sacks. In 1988, he threw 606 passes and was sacked just six times. In 1993, he tore his Achilles tendon and ended a streak of 145 consecutive games played. In 1994, this Miami icon played himself in the movie *Ace Ventura: Pet Detective.* The *Sporting News* list of the NFL's top 100 players of all time includes Marino as number 27.

He's nice, he's always around, he always gives us hugs, every day right after school he gives us hugs and kisses.

—Ali

*As time goes on and I realize I have a teen-
ager, it hits you all of a sudden and you realize you have got to spend as much time as
you can with them. You MAKE TIME—as
much as you can.*

—DAN

Ivan 'Pudge" Rodriguez Derrick & Amanda

*The time that I am not working I want
to spend with the kids because now is
the time that you can be with them.
When they get big they'll want to do
their own thing.*

—IVAN

Ivan: *I'm not your favorite player?*
Who's your favorite player?
Derrick: *Derek Jeter because he*
plays shortstop and I play shortstop.
Ivan: *They are great kids. They make*
me laugh a lot.

Amanda: *What do you love the most about me?*
Ivan: *I love everything about you.*
Amanda: *What do you think about my singing?*
Ivan: *That you've got a very, very beautiful voice.*

Ivan Rodriguez, born November 30, 1971, is an outstanding catcher in Major League Baseball history and will be an almost certain first-ballot Hall of Famer five years after his career ends. Rodriguez, a career Texas Ranger known as "The Man with the Golden Arm," threw out more than half of all the base stealers both in 1998 and 1999, the highest percentage by far since the league began keeping records of it in 1989. Rodriguez was named the American League MVP in 1999, when he batted .332 with 35 homers, 113 runs batted in, 116 runs scored, and 25 stolen bases. Only 34 runners stole a base on him, and he stole 25 himself. What's also remarkable about Rodriguez is that he combines his defensive skills (eight consecutive Gold Gloves for defensive excellence) with his amazing offensive consistency. He finished the 1990s with five straight seasons of .300, and his nine-year lifetime average is exactly .300. "Pudge" set the record in 1996 for most doubles by a catcher (47) and is the only backstop to get 40 plus twice. The Rangers made the playoffs three times in four seasons in the late 1990s. Rodriguez got married and was called up to the big leagues on the same day in June 1991.

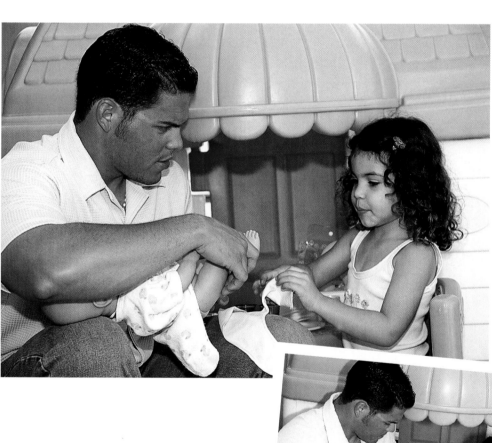

Brett Favre
Brittany & Breleigh

When I go to school he'll drop me off at the bus stop and he gives me a big hug and a big kiss. Sometimes I think, "Oh, that was SO embarrassing."

—BRITTANY

Brett Favre, born October 10, 1969, led the Green Bay Packers to back-to-back Super Bowls, including a victory in Super Bowl XXXI. He replaced an injured Don Majkowski in week three of the 1992 season, and started every game for the next eight years—a record number of consecutive starts by a quarterback. And Favre was the first three-time MVP. He was the NFL's Most Valuable Player in 1995, and again in 1996. In 1997, Favre was co-MVP with Barry Sanders. Favre is quoted as saying, "In order to experience the highs and be in the position I am today, I had to go though a lot of lows." Only two quarterbacks—Steve Young and Joe Montana—have higher career passing ratings than Favre. In Super Bowl XXXI, Favre threw two touchdowns and ran for another, leading the Packers to their first NFL Championship in 29 years. In the 1999 season, Brett engineered three comeback victories in the last minute of the game. Still in mid-career, Favre will challenge the career numbers of the all-time great quarterbacks in history.

He gives me the attention I need and Breleigh the attention she needs. I can take care of myself, but Breleigh needs a lot more help from him.

—BRITTANY

I've come home after throwing four interceptions and Brittany says, "Good game, Daddy." WOW! You know Brittany could care less how many interceptions I throw or touchdowns.

—Brett

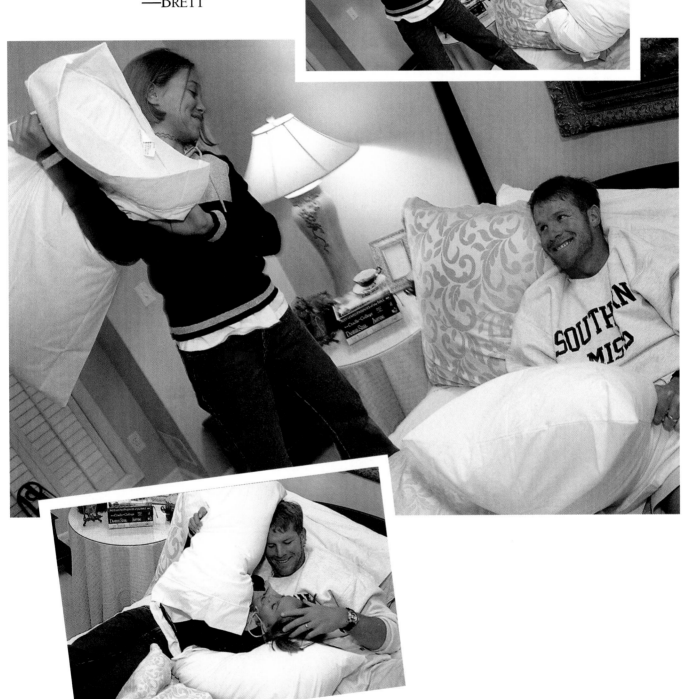

Scott Stevens
Kaitlin, Ryan & Kara

He always takes us fishing. Sometimes we go fishing for fish, and sometimes just for fun. We know how because our daddy taught us. His uncle Mike taught him.

—RYAN

Scott Stevens, born April 1, 1964, has been one of the NHL's best defensemen for almost two decades. He was selected by the Washington Capitals as underage junior in first round (fifth overall pick) of NHL entry draft June 9, 1982. He played eight seasons with the Caps, and holds their all–time record for most penalty minutes (1,630). He signed with the St. Louis Blues as a free agent for the 1990–91 season. Awarded to the New Jersey Devils as compensation for the Blues signing free agent winger Brendan Shanahan, Stevens has played nine seasons with the Devils. He served as captain of the Devils 1992–93 and 1995–96 to present. The highlight of Stevens's career is the 1995 Stanley Cup Championship with New Jersey. He was named to the NHL All Rookie team in 1983, and named to the NHL All-Star first team in the 1987–88 and 1993–94 seasons. He played in the NHL All-Star Game in 1985, 1989, 1991–94, and 1996–98. He was a member of the Canadian team in the 1998 Winter Olympics, and finished with the NHL's best plus-minus rating in 1994 (+53).

He always finds enough time to spend time with us. We go camping and we also like to jump on the water trampoline together. It's really fun. Daddy always bounces us off because he weighs so much.

—KAITLIN

Dan Jansen, born June 17, 1965, is a world class speed skater whose performance at the 1994 Winter Olympics in Lillehammer, Norway, earned him a gold medal for the 1,000 meter and set a new world record. He is the winner of more than thirty World Cup races and more than fifty World Cup medals. In 1984, as an 18-year-old at his first Olympics, Dan finished fourth in the 500 meters, .16 seconds away from a bronze medal. The favored speed skater at the 1988 games in Calgary, Canada, Dan needed all the courage he could gather when, on the day he was to race in the 500 meters, his sister Jane died from leukemia. That evening Dan fell, just 100 meters into the race. He fell again four days later in the 1,000 meter race. The 1992 Winter Olympics brought more disappointment as Dan finished fourth in the 500 meters and 26th in the 1,000. Dan's last shot at the elusive gold medal was in 1994 in Lillehammer. After slipping in the 500, his last Olympic race came in the 1,000 meters, where he finally won the gold. He took his victory lap with his baby Jane in his arms, and as the national anthem played and the American flag rose in front of him, Jansen stood with the gold medal and saluted, "This is for you, Jane. I love you." He was the winner of the 1994 Sullivan Award. Since then, he has established the Dan Jansen Foundation, which contributes primarily to amateur speed skating and the National Leukemia Society.

I would do anything for my daughters. Being with them is the best thing in the world. They are just so sweet. Sometimes when I think about how much they mean to me and how much they've added to my life, I just can't believe it. Nothing else compares.

—DAN

Dan Jansen
Jane & Olivia

Shoo fly don't bother me
Shoo fly don't bother me
Shoo fly don't bother me
I feel like a morning star.

Daddy, you're my drum.

—OLIVIA

Gary Gait
Braden & Taylor

Gary Gait was born in Victoria, British Columbia on April 5, 1967. He is arguably the best all-around lacrosse player in the history of the game and has the MVP awards to prove it. Gait has won three world championships in the Major Indoor Lacrosse League and National Lacrosse League. He has also been named the MVP of those leagues for the past five years (1995–99) and has been named MVP for each of the nine years he has played professionally (1991–99). Gait has won two U.S. Club Lacrosse Association Championships and has been named MVP four times ('93,'95,'96,'97). Gait has won three Canadian National Championships—with the Brooklyn Redmen in 1990 and with the Victoria Shamrocks in 1997 and 1999. While at Syracuse University, Gait led his team to National Championships in 1988, 1989, and 1990. Two years, 1988 and 1990, he was named NCAA Player of the Year. As an assistant coach for the University of Maryland's women's team, Gait's teams won NCAA Championships in 1995, 1996, 1997, 1998, and 1999. Recently, Gary Gait was chosen as one of *CNN Sports Illustrated*'s Top 50 Canadian Athletes of the Century. Currently, Gary plays professional lacrosse in the NLL for the Pittsburgh Crossfire and field lacrosse in the USCLA for Team Toyota. Gary Gait and his identical twin brother own and operate several well-regarded lacrosse camps.

*It's fun to introduce them to all sorts of things—
sports, dance, et cetera every day of the week.
Braden just signed up for his first karate class, so now
that's karate, tap dancing, and swimming for him.*

—GARY

53

He never made me go into golf just because it's what
he does and I really appreciate that. I'm more into
drama—so that's what I do, musicals and plays.
And he tries to support me in whatever I do.

—PAUL

Tom Kite
Stephanie, Paul & David

He's just a good person. I like being around him.

—STEPHANIE

Tom Kite, born December 9, 1949, began the 1999 season as the PGA Tour's third all-time leading money winner. He was the first in tour history to reach $6 million, $7 million, $8 million, and $9 million dollars in career earnings. Of his 19 PGA Tour victories, his most memorable was the 1992 U.S. Open at Pebble Beach. His even par 72 in difficult Sunday conditions earned him a two-stroke victory over Jeff Sluman to give him the Open. He turned pro in 1972, after sharing the NCAA title with Ben Crenshaw. He was the tour's Rookie of the Year in 1973, and competed for the United States in seven Ryder Cups before captaining the team in 1997. Kite was the PGA Player of the Year in 1989, and was the tour's all-time leading earner from 1989 to 1995. A new wave of stars would emerge, and in 1997, Kite would finish second to Tiger Woods at the 1997 Masters. He is one of the greatest golfers ever from the state of Texas, which is saying a lot.

Sometimes people meet us and expect us to all play golf, or be snobs about it because golf has such a stuffy reputation. What we do is just get rid of that stereotype.

—PAUL

Terry Porter

Brianna, Franklin & Malcolm

*My kids are so important to me. It's hard to describe
how much I love them and how much better they can
make me feel just by being with them. There are
times when I come home from a game where I haven't
played that well, and they say, "Good job, Daddy"
and I realize THEY are what is most important.*

—TERRY

I love my dad because he's nice and fun and funny. When I want to do something special for him, I tell him to go golfing.

—BRIANNA

I have been on the receiving end of water guns many times.

—TERRY

Terry Porter, born April 8, 1963, is one of the finest NBA point guards of his generation. He played college ball at tiny Wisconsin–Stevens Point, and was the 24th pick in the 1985 NBA draft. Selected by the Portland Trailblazers, Porter started eight seasons for the Blazers, leading a great backcourt that included Clyde Drexler. Porter finished in the top five in assists for three straight seasons in the late eighties. Porter raised his scoring average to a career-high 18.2 points per game in 1993. Terry has always been a great defender, especially in stealing the ball. He finished ninth in the 1991 MVP voting, and is a two-time All Star. He went to the Minnesota Timberwolves as a free agent prior to the 1996 season, and tutored the young Stephon Marbury in 1997. He was invaluable for the Miami Heat in 1999, and in the 2000 season he joined the NBA champion San Antonio Spurs to replace injured starter Sean Elliott. He's appeared in 92 playoff games, including 11 finals games in 1990 and 1992. He's in the top 12 players for most career three-pointers, and only John Stockton and Derek Harper have played more games as point guards. An iron man, Porter has played every game on the schedule in six different seasons, and in 15 years had only one year where he missed any more than three contests. He was the winner of the 1993 J. Walter Kennedy Citizenship Award.

Tino Martinez
Olivia, TJ & Victoria

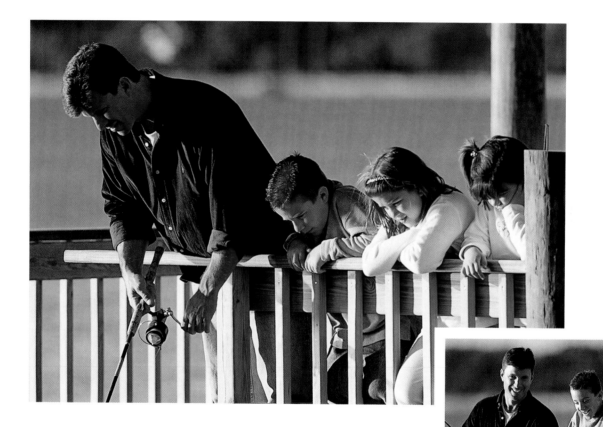

I think my dad is a superhero.

—TJ

*I try the best I can on off days
from baseball to fly home to see
them and take them to school
and whatnot. I try to have a
real active role in it and let
them know that I am their dad
before I am a baseball player.*
—TINO

Tino Martinez, born December 7, 1967, is a left-handed-hitting first baseman for the New York Yankees. In his first four seasons with New York, he was a part of three World Series Championships, including a record-breaking 1998 season. Tino was an All American at the University of Tampa, and in 1988 he led the U.S. Olympic team to a gold medal at the Seoul Olympics. He was selected by the Seattle Mariners in the first round of the 1988 draft, and played his first five seasons with the Mariners. He was traded by the Mariners to the Yankees on his 28th birthday, and replaced longtime Yankee first baseman Don Mattingly. He is a two-time All Star (1995 with Seattle and 1997 with New York). His career season came in 1997, when he was second in the American League in home runs and RBIs. He finished the season with 44 homers and 141 RBIs. He finished the 1990s with five consecutive 100 RBI seasons. In his first post-season series, against the Yankees in 1995, Martinez batted .409 with a homer and 5 RBIs in the five games. For New York, Tino's greatest postseason moment came in Game One of the 1998 World Series. Tino's sixth inning grand slam led the Yankees to a come-from-behind win. Another World Series sweep in 1999 meant Tino and the Yankees had won 12 consecutive World Series games—the last four games of 1996, and sweeps in 1998 and 1999.

My friends love him. I love him. I love when he pushes me on the swings. I love when he goes in the pool with me. He helps me with my homework. Some of my homework is really confusing. My dad can't figure it out or me either.

—OLIVIA

Dominik Hasek
Michael & Dominika

I love my dad this much. I love him as big as an elephant.

—DOMINIKA

Dominik Hasek, born January 29, 1965, is one of the leading goalies in the National Hockey League. A native of Pardubice, Czechoslovakia, Hasek was selected by the Chicago Blackhawks in the tenth round of the 1983 NHL entry draft. After two seasons with Chicago, Hasek was traded to the Buffalo Sabres on August 7, 1992. In the eight plus seasons since, he has been among the league's best goalies. He was a gold medal winner for the Czech Republic Olympic team in 1998. And he holds virtually all the Buffalo team records for a goalie, including games played, shutouts, and goals against average. Nicknamed "the Dominator," Hasek is a two-time winner of the Hart Trophy (MVP), and became the first goaltender to win back-to-back Hart Trophies (1997, 1998). In 1996–97, Hasek became the first netminder to capture the Hart Trophy since Jacques Plante of the Montreal Canadiens in 1962. The premiere goalie in the NHL with five Vezina Trophy awards in a six-year period, he announced in the Czech Republic in July, 1999, that he would retire after the 1999–00 season to spend more time with his family. He then forfeited the final year of his three-year, $26 million contract (over $9 million). Hasek led the Sabres to the Stanley Cup Finals in the spring of 1999, a season that saw him go 30–18–14 with a 1.87 goals against average. In the postseason, he was 13-6 with a 1.77 goals against average. Hasek has led the NHL in save percentage each of six consecutive seasons. Although he was out with an injury for the 1999–00 season, he was named as a starter in the 2000 All Star game.

Tony Meola was born on February 21, 1969, in Belleville, New Jersey; his parents came from Avellino, Italy. Tony earned his first honor in high school: the New Jersey state title of 1986. He was an All-America goalkeeper with 43 shutouts. In his senior year, he played forward and scored 33 goals! The New York Yankees wanted to draft Tony right out of high school, but he wanted a career in soccer. So he went to the University of Virginia on a soccer/baseball scholarship. In 1987 he started for the United States in the U–20 World Cup in Chile. In his sophomore year, he dropped out to get a spot on the 1990 World Cup team. Only days before he was in goal for the United States' 1–0 victory in Trinidad & Tobago, qualifying them for their first World Cup in 40 years, he was named winner of the Hermann Trophy, given to the top college player in the States. He played in all three games of the 1990 World Cup and all four in 1994 as well as being the 1994 team captain. After the World Cup, Tony tried out as a placekicker for the New York Jets, but he was cut. In the winter of '95 he played with an indoor league team, the Buffalo Blizzards. He played his first and last season with the Long Island Rough Riders in 1995, when they won their league championship. Since then, he has starred with the New York/New Jersey Metrostars and the Kansas City Wizards. Tony also has co-starred in an off-Broadway play called *Tony n' Tina's Wedding,* and he plays drums in a band called Mushmouth.

Tony Meola
Jonathan

*We're at such a neat stage right now.
He's learning to talk. He communicates
so well. It is great to see him make
his own decisions—totally unforced
and unrehearsed.*

—TONY

I definitely spend more time teaching my son to be tender than to be tough. He is naturally going to run into walls and try to run other kids over.

—TONY

Junior Seau
Sydney & Jake

I would like to prepare them to deal with disappointment. You can't expect everything to come easily and I want them to be prepared to handle those types of difficulties.

—JUNIOR

*I pray to God that Daddy
is safe and doesn't get hurt
playing football.*

—SYDNEY

*When I grow up I want to be an artist,
a surfer. I want to be everything—
everything but a football player—
DEFINITELY NOT a football player.*

—Sydney

I don't know how to read,
Daddy reads to us.

—JAKE

My biggest worry is the children's physical safety.

—JUNIOR

Junior Seau was born January 19, 1969, and moved to American Samoa at an early age. Moving back to the mainland before grade school, Seau did not speak English until age seven. Today he is known as one of the best linebackers in NFL history. He has played his entire pro career in San Diego, and he is one of the most recognizable figures in the area. He is arguably the greatest player ever to play for the Chargers. In his first nine seasons, he started 140 out of 141 games. He was the fifth pick in the 1990 draft. Averaging close to 120 tackles per season, Seau has played most of his career as an inside linebacker; at various times, he has played outside linebacker and middle linebacker. His play in 1998 was spectacular, leading the Chargers to the number one ranking in the league in defense (fewest yards allowed). But his career season probably came in 1994, when he led the Chargers to their first-ever Super Bowl appearance. In that season, Seau had 155 tackles, 5.5 sacks, one forced fumble, and three fumble recoveries. In the AFC Championship game, Seau led the Chargers to an improbable road victory that sent his team to the Super Bowl. Junior had 16 tackles and helped limit the Steelers to just 66 yards rushing in a hard-fought 17–13 win. In 1999, the Chargers used him sparingly at tight end and half back. He will one day, without doubt, be enshrined in Canton in the Pro Football Hall of Fame.

Richard Petty

Kyle, Sharon, Lisa & Rebecca

They were little bitty things when we first started taking them to races with us. Our kids had all of the regular kids' things happen to them, but a lot of the time they happened at the races.

—RICHARD

*No matter what was going on in Daddy's
life, he would always go around the table
at dinner and talk to each one of us about
what was going on in school.*

—Rebecca

I was in the third grade before I realized that everybody's parents didn't have race cars.

—KYLE

Richard Petty, known as "The King," was born June 2, 1937. Over the course of 32 years driving on the NASCAR Winston Cup circuit and a record 200 victories, The King has seen his sport grow from the dirt tracks of North Carolina to the brand-new speedways and multimillion-dollar national television contracts. Many would argue that Petty was the guiding force that turned NASCAR racing into the most popular form of motor sports in America today. His numbers are remarkable: 200 wins (at his retirement, no one else had more than 105) and seven Winston Cup championships. Petty won seven Daytona 500 races, the first in 1964, the last in 1981. He had 41 five-hundred-mile wins and 27 wins in a single season (1967), winning ten races in a row that year. He had at least one victory every season for 18 years (1960–77) and purses totaling nearly $8 million dollars. Petty remains the most beloved figure in NASCAR history. Nine times he won the Most Popular Driver award. He received the Medal of Freedom, the highest U.S. civilian award, in 1992. Since his retirement from competitive driving in 1992, he has not stopped trying to win races. Petty Enterprises is responsible for two Winston Cup teams, and a NASCAR Craftsman Truck Series race truck. As Richard followed his father, Lee, his son, Kyle, followed Richard, and now his sons, Adam and Austin, are following their father. Four generations of Pettys—now that is a dynasty!

Kyle Petty, born June 2, 1960, is a professional race car driver, grandson of racing legend Lee Petty (the 1959 Daytona 500 winner) and son of seven-time Winston Cup Champion Richard "The King" Petty. Kyle's "Charity Ride" has raised more than $1.5 million in its five years; his food drives have provided thousands of meals for people who otherwise would go hungry. Recognized as a gentleman both on and off the track, Petty, driver of the #44 Petty Enterprises Hot Wheels Pontiac, is one of the most popular drivers. Kyle has more than 150 top 10 finishes, and has earned more than $10 million dollars in his career. In 1986, he won his first Winston Cup event, becoming the first third-generation driver to win. In 1992, Kyle became the first Petty to win $1 million dollars in one season. He finished fifth in NASCAR Winston Cup points that year. In 1993, he won the pole position for the Daytona 500 by STP and finished fifth in NASCAR Winston Cup points. Kyle's relationship with Hot Wheels has allowed him to give back to some of his "biggest" fans: children. In 1997, Kyle joined his father, Richard, and engine builder David Evans to form Petty Enterprises 2, a Winston Cup team fielding the #44 Hot Wheels Pontiac Grand Prix. He joined forces with his father again in Randleman, North Carolina, to host the #43 and #44 Winston Cup race teams. Kyle was selected by *NASCAR Winston Cup Illustrated* as its 1999 Person of the Year. He's been called the world's coolest race car driver. The Petty family's 50-year racing legacy will continue with Kyle's sons, Adam and Austin.

Kyle Petty

The one conscious effort we have made over the years is that every night before we go to bed we all gather in our bedroom and we all say our prayers.

—KYLE

Adam, Austin & Montgomery Lee

He's a thirty-nine-year-old with the personality of a twelve-year-old. He's very childlike.

—AUSTIN

He's really nice and I just love him to death. He's a little kid all the time.
— Montgomery

Michael Weiss
Annie Mae

I know that the most important thing I can do for my children is spend time with them. I would like our children to grow up knowing how important they are to us.

—Michael

*Annie Mae is so funny. She's really outgoing
and always likes to talk to people wherever
we go. They are usually surprised when she
says hello to them because she is so young.*

— MICHAEL

Kids should have the freedom to be able to feel good about themselves. They should be judged individually, not on how they compare with other people.

—MICHAEL

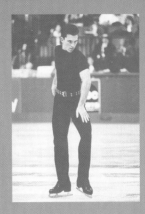

Michael Weiss, born August 2, 1976, is one of the best male figure skaters in the world. His list of accomplishments is long and distinguished. After placing second two years in a row at the U.S. National Championships, Weiss earned his ranking as the top U.S. skater at the 1999 Championships in Salt Lake City. Later in the year, he earned the bronze medal at the World Championships in Helsinki. He is currently a featured skater in the popular John Hancock Champions on Ice tour. He started skating when he was nine, after having accompanied his older sister to her ice skating training sessions. His parents once owned a gymnastics school in Olney, Maryland, and his father was a member of the 1964 U.S. Olympic gymnastics team. His mother was also a competitive gymnast. Older sisters Genna and Geremi also competed in diving and figure skating. Weiss's signature moves include the walley-reverse, walley-triple Lutz combination, triple Lutz landing with arms in reverse position, and backflip. He hopes to be the first American to land a quad in competition. When in preparation for competition, Weiss works out five days a week and—unlike most skaters—makes weight training a regular part of his workout. He has bench pressed an impressive 300 pounds, nearly twice his weight.

Greg LeMond
Geoffrey, Scott & Simone

I would love my children to understand that if you live your life as honestly and ethically as possible, you'll never have to compromise your values.

—Greg

Our number one goal is to bring up kids who have compassion for others and do not believe that they are any better than anyone else.

—GREG

Greg LeMond, born in 1961, is considered the greatest American cyclist of all time. As a three-time winner of the Tour de France and a three-time cycling world champion, Greg reestablished the United States as a source of world-class cyclists. He has been named *Sports Illustrated*'s Sportsman of the Year (1989), and one of *Sports Illustrated*'s 40 most influential athletic figures over the last 40 years. LeMond started competitive cycling at age 14 and he turned pro at 19. In 1983, he became the first American to win the professional road race at the world championships. In 1984, LeMond became the second American ever to attempt the Tour de France, finishing third. In 1985, he finished second in the Tour. Then, in 1986, LeMond became the first non-European ever to win. But in April, 1987, LeMond went turkey hunting and an accidental shotgun blast almost cost LeMond his life. He survived but the accident cost him two years of his career. His goal for the 1989 Tour de France was to finish in the top 20. Then on July 23, the last day of the Tour, he trailed France's Laurent Fignon by 50 seconds, a margin considered too considerable to erase in the final time trial. With the fastest time trial in history, LeMond beat Fignon by eight seconds in what was hailed as the most exciting Tour finish ever. LeMond won the Tour de France for the third time in 1990. After retiring in 1995, he has pursued a career as a race car driver in the Formula Ford 2000 series.

Bill Walton

Luke, Nathan, Adam & Chris

It's the mealtimes, it's the long walks in the parks, it's going out to shoot baskets, taking them to the movies, just being with them. We used to go on trips together when they were a lot younger. Now they just want my credit card, my keys, and my cell phone.

—BILL

Bill Walton, born November 5, 1952, was one of the greatest basketball players of all time. At UCLA, his teams won a record 88 consecutive games, and he was voted the NCAA Player of the Year twice. He won the Sullivan Award as 1973's Best Amateur Athlete. He was the first overall pick in the 1974 NBA Draft (by the Portland Trailblazers). Injuries cut short his NBA career—but not before Bill won the MVP in 1978 and led the Blazers to the 1977 NBA Championship. After a series of leg injuries, Walton was able to come back with the Boston Celtics playing a key role, winning the NBA's sixth Man Award on the 1986 Championship team. Fans today remember Walton for his left-wing politics: in college, he sent President Nixon a letter asking for his resignation, and it is jokingly said that Walton attended Grateful Dead concerts more often than he played in NBA games! Since 1990, the outspoken redhead has been an accomplished broadcaster with NBC Sports. He was chosen as one of the 50 Greatest Players in NBA History in 1997 during the league's 50th anniversary celebration.

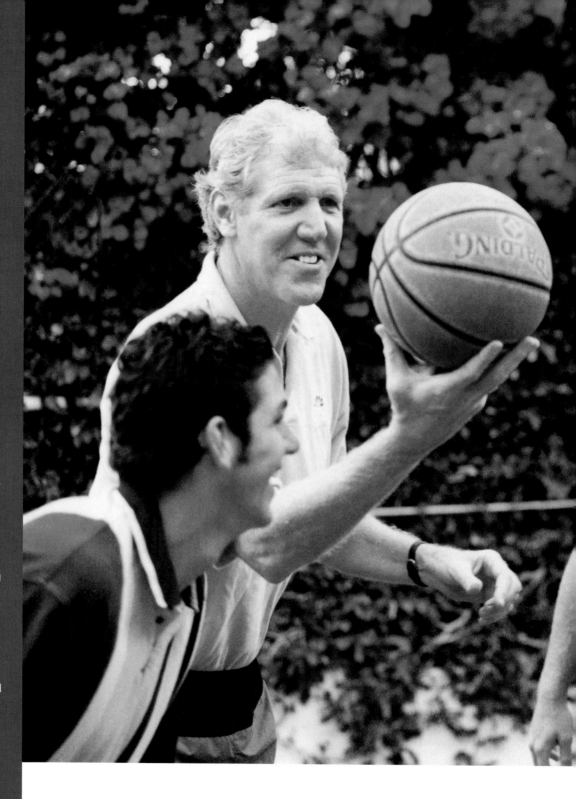

I learned from my parents and from my great coaches and teachers that leading by example is the best form of teaching and if you're not there on a daily basis, it's definitely more challenging.

—BILL

It's the personal contact that's so essential in the long-term teaching of your kids.

—BILL

Scott Tinley
Torrie & Dane

Fatherhood keeps everything in perspective. If you're going to do your job as a parent, then that is ultimately much more important than any adulation you receive as an athlete.

—SCOTT

Scott Tinley has been competing in the sport of triathlon since its inception in 1976. He has competed in more than 400 events and won close to 100 of them, making him one of the top three most successful triathletes of all time. Additionally, he finished in the top three a record 30 times at the Ironman, the European Championship (Nice, France), and the USTS Nationals. He won the Ironman Triathlon in Hawaii twice, the Ironman World Series three times and has raced in more than twenty countries around the world. Tinley was inducted into the Ironman Hall of Fame in 1996. He helped launch and manage the successful Tinley Performancewear Line of active clothing in 1984 and eventually sold the company to Reebok, Intl. in 1992. He has also authored four books on multisport and lifestyle training and has been a freelance writer for Triathlete Magazine, Men's Journal, and Men's Fitness. He has also acted as cohost for Triathlete Magazine on TV, and has been a marketing consultant for such companies as PowerFood, Timex, and Litespeed bicycles. His quest for new and challenging opportunities has led him to adventure racing and a sport he practically invented, off-road triathlon. He remains competitive in these fields even in his forties and was invited to compete in NBC's Survival of the Fittest and Superstars Competition.

*My dad and I like to go to
some property where there's
lots of dirt—we take walks,
hang out, and talk a lot.*

—DANE

Reggie White
Jeremy & Jocolia

Being a father is the most rewarding relationship in my life other than my relationship with God.

—REGGIE

Reggie White, born December 19, 1961, is the NFL's all-time leading sack leader with 165.5. He was named to the NFL's 75th Anniversary All-Time team in August 1994. He tied a record with 11 consecutive appearances in the Pro Bowl. He sacked an astounding 62 different quarterbacks. The highlight of his career was being on the Super Bowl Champion Packers team in January 1997. Naturally, White had three sacks to lead the Packers over the Patriots in the Super Bowl. Reggie began his professional career with the United States Football League's Memphis Showboats. He joined the NFL's Philadelphia Eagles in 1985, and spent eight seasons there. After that, White was a free agent and said he wanted to go wherever he felt God wanted him to go. The man known as the "Minister of Defense" chose Green Bay, and finished his career as a Packer, playing with them for eight years. When White was seventeen, he received his minister's license from St. John's Baptist Church. Then in 1992, he was ordained as a nondenominational minister. He is president of Big Doggie records and copastor of the Inner City Church of East Knoxville, Tennessee.

He always gets along so well with all sorts of people. If there's one thing he's taught me, it is to always be kind to everyone.

—JOCOLIA

When my son, Jeremy, was born, I started
crying because God had blessed me with a
son. I cried just as hard when my daughter,
Jocolia, was born. I was so thankful to
God for my family.

—REGGIE

*My dad's willing to talk about
things . . . he always wants us to
be open with him.*

—JEREMY

Keith Van Horn
Sabrina & Nicholas

*Fatherhood has been great. It's been the
most eye-opening experience I've been
through. It changed my life dramatically.*

—KEITH

My daddy takes me on dates. We go to
his basketball practices. I get to color when
I go to practice with him. Sometimes I make
pictures for my dad and sometimes I make
pictures for his big friends.

—SABRINA

Keith Van Horn, born October 23, 1975, is a 6'10" forward in the NBA who starred for four years at the University of Utah. Following his career at Utah, Van Horn was the second player chosen in the 1998 NBA Draft and was traded from Philadelphia to New Jersey in an eight-player deal shortly after the draft. Van Horn led the Nets in scoring as a rookie, earned a berth on the NBA's All-Rookie First Team and finished second to the Spurs' Tim Duncan in the balloting for Rookie of the Year. He did even better in his second season with the Nets, finishing fifth in the NBA in scoring with 21.8 points per game. The Nets signed Van Horn to a six-year, $73 million dollar extension in the summer of 1999, which puts him under contract to the year 2006. Van Horn and center Jayson Williams have managed to bring a national appeal to the Nets. In an extraordinary collegiate career at the University of Utah, Van Horn earned first-team All-America honors after his senior season, was a three-time Western Athletic Conference (WAC) Player of the Year, was the top scorer in Utah and WAC history with 2,542 points, and averaged 20.8 points and 8.8 rebounds per game over his four years at the school. Keith Van Horn is only the fifth player in University of Utah history to have his number, 44, retired.

I hope that they will grow up to be happy individuals. I just want them to grow up to do something they love doing.

—K<small>EITH</small>

Howie Long
Chris, Kyle & Howie

*I'm constantly trying to improve: improve my patience,
not saying the first thing that pops into my mind,
realizing that all three of them are totally different
and they all present different challenges.*

—HOWIE

Howie Long, born January 6, 1960, was one of the greatest Los Angeles Raider players of all time. Long, a former defensive end, joined the Oakland Raiders as a second round draft choice (48th overall) from Villanova. He became a starter in his second season (the Raiders' first in Los Angeles) and led them to an 8–1 mark in a strike-shortened year. The following year Long posted 13 sacks, including 5 in one game, and the Raiders enjoyed a championship season, defeating the Washington Redskins in Super Bowl XVIII. Long went to eight Pro Bowls, tying the then franchise record, and was named first team defensive end on the All-NFL team of the 1980s. For the ten-year period from 1982–1992, Long's 78 sacks ranked fifth best in the NFL, trailing the great Lawrence Taylor. Playing at 6'5", 275 pounds, Long combined strength with speed and explosive quickness. He capped his pro football career with an induction into the Football Hall of Fame in 2000. And Long always had excellent timing: Villanova voluntarily disbanded its football program immediately after his senior year, the Raiders would stay in Los Angeles only one more season following Howie's retirement and a new NFL television contract in 1994 opened the door for Long to join Fox Sports as a studio analyst. Long's work for Fox earned considerable praise, including an Emmy Award in 1997. And in addition to sports television, Long has branched out to become a screen star in the action-adventure films *Broken Arrow* and *Firestorm*.

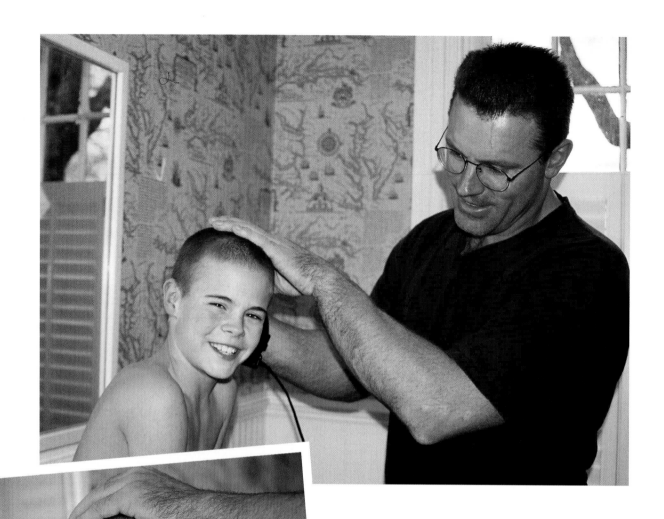

I think my dad is the best
in the world. When I'm a dad
and try to be a good dad I'll
do everything my dad did.

—Howie

People would be surprised that I beat him up. He's really small, he's weak. My special plan is to kick him and run.

—CHRIS

When I'm sad, he tries to cheer me up and then he tells me not to smile and then I end up smiling and laughing and he comes up to me and tickles me and then we have a wrestling match.

—K<small>YLE</small>

Orel Hershiser, born September 16, 1958, has pitched 17 years in the Major Leagues, the first twelve with the Los Angeles Dodgers, and has won more than 200 games. In 1985, Hershiser had a 19–3 record and a 2.03 ERA, and won his last 11 games of the season. But his greatest season came in 1988: he won 23 games, the most by a Dodgers pitcher since Sandy Koufax won 27 in 1966. He had a record-setting 59 consecutive scoreless innings. He was named Sportsman of the Year by Sports Illustrated, A.P. Male Athlete of the Year, the National League Championship series MVP, and World Series MVP. He shut out the Mets in game seven of the NLCS to advance Los Angeles to the World Series, and clinched it with a complete game. Major shoulder surgery in 1990 meant a yearlong rehabilitation, and Hershiser won Comeback Player of the Year in 1991. In addition, he has won Gold Gloves as a fielder, batted .356 in the 1993 season to win the Silver Slugger Award (for best-hitting pitcher) and in the late 1990s was frequently mentioned as a future managerial candidate. In 1995, Hershiser won 16 games for the Cleveland Indians and won MVP of the American League Championship Series. He pitched _____ for the Indians

If the love that you show them can transfer over to their siblings and they can treat each other with love and respect, then you've got some kind of family.

—OREL

Orel Hershiser
Quinton & Jordan

*He's cheesy most of the time, he's funny
some of the time. He tries to make jokes
but he's not always funny.*

—JORDAN

He's definitely the role model of the
family. He always sets the standard.
He's reasonable—he always hears us
out first and then shares his opinion.

—QUINTON

When **Peter Vidmar** was 11 years old, his parents found an ad in the newspaper for a new "experimental gymnastics program designed to develop future Olympic champions." They brought Peter to the gym and Makoto Sakamoto, the former Olympian who ran the ad, made good on his promise. For the next 12 years Makoto and Peter practiced and practiced. In 1979, Vidmar attended his first World Championships in Fort Worth, Texas; there the Americans finished a solid sixth. Vidmar then earned a spot on the 1980 Olympic team, but the boycott left his Olympic dreams unfulfilled. At the 1981 World Championships, the U.S. men, with Vidmar to help guide them, moved up to fifth place. In 1983 the U.S. edged up one more notch to fourth and Vidmar entered the world's top ten, finishing ninth. At the 1984 Olympic Games in Los Angeles, Peter Vidmar established himself not only as one of the world's great gymnasts, but as an inspirational force as well. Vidmar captained the U.S. men's gymnastics team to its first-ever Olympic Gold Medal in a stunning upset victory over the defending world champions from the People's Republic of China. Today he spends much of his time as a leader and motivator to business audiences across the nation. *Successful Meetings* magazine listed him as one of the top ten corporate speakers in America.

Peter Vidmar

Timothy, Christopher, Stephen, Kathryn & Emily

*I often quote a famous theologian:
"The greatest work that you'll ever do
in your life will be within the confines
of your own home and no success in
life can compensate for failure in your
home." That's my life's motto.*

—PETER

John Starks
John Jr. & Chelsea

I love my dad. He's a good basketball player. Someday, I want to play basketball just like him but on a women's team.

—CHELSEA

John Starks, born August 10, 1965, is one of the NBA's most fiery competitors and shooters as well as one of the NBA's greatest success stories. He played basketball only one season (junior year) at Central High School in Tulsa. He played for four colleges in four years and was never drafted by an NBA franchise. Cut by the Golden State Warriors in 1989, he played in the CBA in the 1989–90 season. He was signed by the Knicks as a free agent on October 1, 1990 and has since become an NBA fixture. He was named to the 1994 All-Star game. He is known for one of the most memorable plays in playoff history with .47 seconds remaining in Game Two of the 1993 Eastern Conference finals against Chicago with a driving lefthanded dunk. He averaged 17.7 points per game in the 1994 NBA finals against the Houston Rockets. Starks shares an NBA playoff record with six three-pointers made in a half, against Indiana in 1995. In 1997, Starks won the NBA Sixth Man Award. And he became a real fan favorite in New York, where he played alongside Charles Oakley and Patrick Ewing for eight seasons. Following the 1998 season, he was included in the trade to Golden State for Latrell Sprewell. Starks went from obscurity to All-Star, then withstood all the pressures to have a long and productive NBA career.

Fatherhood is a process you grow into. I feel blessed to have my children.

—JOHN

I like going places with my dad, like playing golf—it's also fun to play basketball together in our backyard.

—JOHN JR.

Shane Sellers

Shali, Saban & Steiner

Sometimes when he comes home, he'll run up to us and hug us and he'll start hugging us so tight that we can't get away.

—SHALI

Shane Sellers, born September 24, 1966, is one of the leading jockeys in the country. The Louisville, Kentucky, resident was one of the top five money earners in 1999, having ridden more than 200 winners, including Vicar in the Florida Derby. Earnings of $12,887,304 dollars placed him eighth on the national list in 1998, winning 252 races. In 1997, he ranked sixth nationally when he rode 280 winners. He began working around horses at age 11 in Louisiana, and scored his first win in 1983 at Evangeline Downs. He won his first Breeders Cup race in 1997 on Countess Diana in the Juvenile Fillies. The fall of 1997 also saw two milestones for Sellers: his three thousandth career win aboard Claiborne Farm and Adele Dilschneider's two-year old colt, Arch, at Kenneland. And he won his sixth riding title at Kenneland that fall. His best Triple Crown showing came in 1993, when he finished third in both the Kentucky Derby and the Belmont Stakes on Wild Gale. He rode Skip Away to victory over Cigar in the 1996 Jockey Club Gold Cup. The 5'3" father of three is also a budding country music singer.

Steiner can be an actress. She
can turn on the tears at the
drop of a hat, and every time
it breaks my heart.

    —SHANE

They know that I'm going to lay down the law. They understand that's part of being a dad. Once we straighten things out, I let them know how much I love them and give them a big hug.

—SHANE

Doug Flutie
Alexa & Dougie

The best thing about being a father is when you get feedback from the kids—smiles on their faces. That's the stuff that I love.

—Doug

Because of his autism, we have expectations for Dougie in what we think he can achieve but he's got his own list. The things on it are not based on my accomplishments. We want him to reach his fullest potential.

—DOUG

Doug Flutie, born October 23, 1962, has been an outstanding college and pro football quarterback for almost two decades, despite being only 5'9" and 175 pounds. He won the Heisman Trophy in 1984 with Boston College, and has played in the USFL, NFL, and CFL. He was a six-time CFL MVP. Returning to the NFL in 1998, he led the Buffalo Bills into the playoffs two straight seasons. He's best known for a single moment in his final regular season game at Boston College. On November 23, 1984, Flutie's Eagles staged a memorable duel with defending national champions Miami. The game swung back and forth. Down 45–41, the Eagles took over on their own 20 yard line with 28 seconds remaining. Three plays and 22 seconds later, Doug Flutie had one more play; he called for the "Flood Tip," which put three receivers in the same corner of the end zone. Gerard Phelan's reception immortalized Flutie. At the time of his departure from college, Flutie was the all-time NCAA passing leader with 10,759 yards. In 1985, he played for the New Jersey Generals of the USFL. In 1986, he was with the Chicago Bears, playing five games. He wasn't in an NFL system that was right for him in Chicago, or in New England (where he played from 1987–89). But he flourished in Canada, dominating the league. He was the NFL's Comeback Player of the Year in 1998. His hometown of Natick, Massachusetts, has a street named after him—Flutie Pass.

Wayne Gretzky, born January 26, 1961, is one of the most famous athletes of all time. Nicknamed "The Great One," Wayne set 61 NHL scoring records and played in 18 All-Star games in his 21-year career. A native of Canada, Gretzky began skating when he was three years old. His father flooded the back-yard and strung lights for the young Gretzky to skate by at night. He turned pro in 1978, making his debut with the Indianapolis Racers of the World Hockey Association. But in late 1978, his contract was sold to the Edmonton Oilers. The next season, Gretzky became the youngest MVP ever, as well as the youngest in league history to score 50 goals and 100 points in a season. Gretzky led the Oilers to four Stanley Cup Championships in a five year span ('84, '85, '87, '88). In 1982, he scored a record 92 goals in one season. He was traded to the Los Angeles Kings in 1988. Among his records are most career goals (894), most career assists (1,961), most career points (2,855), most points in a single season (215), most career playoff goals (122), and most career All-Star goals (13). He led the league in scor-ing 10 different seasons, and won the Lady Byng Trophy for sportsmanship five different years. In November 1999, the mandatory three-year waiting period was waived and #99 was inducted into the NHL Hall of Fame.

Wayne Gretzky
Pauline, Ty & Trevor

When my kids get up in the morning
and come in and give me a hug and kiss
and say, "Daddy, I love you," there's
nothing that can match it.

—WAYNE

I'm such a softie. When the kids misbehave we give them a time out, which is like going to the penalty box, only it's to their room.

—WAYNE

When I was twenty-three, I never thought about having kids. I felt like I was the kid. I didn't ever think, "Well, in the next three years I'm going to have three kids." Then, overnight, your priorities change, your thoughts change.

—WAYNE

Joe Montana

Alexandra, Elizabeth, Nathaniel & Nicholas

*You hope that you give them a strong foundation—
and that we never ever lose touch with who really
gives support and where the real meaning of life
comes from—your family.*

—JOE

Joe Montana, born June 11, 1956, is considered one of the most respected quarterbacks in NFL history. He led the San Francisco 49ers from 1979–1990 and again in 1992, and finished his career with the Kansas City Chiefs in 1994. Montana led his team to four Super Bowls, all triumphs, and was Most Valuable Player of the Super Bowl three times. Montana engineered a 92-yard drive in the closing minutes of Super Bowl XXIII to defeat the Cincinnati Bengals. Prior to joining the 49ers, Montana played at Notre Dame, where he led the Fighting Irish to the national championship in 1977. He capped his college career by bringing Notre Dame back from a 22-point deficit with five minutes left to win the 1979 Cotton Bowl. Montana came from Monongahela, Pennsylvania. His former mentor and coach with the 49ers, Bill Walsh, said of him, "When the game is on the line, and you need someone to go in there and win it right now, I would rather have Joe Montana as my quarterback than anyone who ever played the game." A scrambling Montana lofted a six-yard pass to the end zone and found Dwight Clark in the 1981 NFC title game that became known simply as "The Catch." In four Super Bowls, Montana threw 11 touchdowns and not a single interception. ESPN selected Montana as the 25th greatest athlete of the 20th century, trailing only Jim Brown among NFL players. He was inducted into the Pro Football Hall of Fame in 2000.

*I've never been very good at going to athletic events.
I don't enjoy watching; I'd rather be playing. But
when I first went to one of Alexandra and Elizabeth's
baseball games, it was the first time I can remember
getting excited as a spectator.*

—JOE

Peter Vermes
Nicole & Kyle

Daddy, why are you always so nice to us?

—NICOLE

Peter Vermes, born January 21, 1966, is one of the most experienced soccer players in U.S. history. Serving as the field general whose instructions can often be heard in the upper stands, he plays for the Kansas City Wizards in the MLS after previously playing for the Colorado Rapids and the MetroStars as well as being an integral part of the U.S. national team (1988–94). Vermes is a midfielder/defender, who has played sweeper, outside back, and even offensive midfielder. His father, Michael, played professionally in Hungary in the 1950s. Two older brothers also played soccer, and helped teach Vermes the game. He attended Delran High School and was named Player of the Year. He played at Rutgers University, then became the first American to play in Hungary's first division and also in Holland's first division. He captained the MetroStars in their inaugural season of 1996, leading the team to the Eastern Conference semifinals. His solid play at the MLS level earned Vermes a recall into the U.S. national team for the final round with a 4–2 win over El Salvador at Foxboro. He started all three games for the United States in the 1990 World Cup in Italy, and represented the United States in the 1988 Olympics in Seoul.

*Once my dad let us dress
him up as a bunny rabbit.*

—KYLE

Nicole was our first child. You spend all that time—the nine months—worrying, then the baby comes and instantaneously you are so attached.

—PETER

When you get to the point where you are very comfortable in what you're doing—it's almost like your perception opens up to things that you have missed. Now I don't bring my sport home with me anymore.

—PETER

John Elway

Jessica, Jack, Jordan & Juliana

*One thing I wish . . . I wish I was as
persistent as they are. Sometimes it
takes ten "no"s for them to listen.*

—JOHN

John Elway, born July 28, 1960, was one of the greatest quarterbacks in NFL history. He played 16 years with the Denver Broncos, leading them to five Super Bowls. He was the most successful starting quarterback in league history (148 victories), but he'll be forever known for winning Super Bowls XXXII and XXXIII at the very end of his 16-year career. His father, Jack, was a college football coach and the family moved a great deal. John chose Stanford University, in part because the school was "the only one that actively encouraged me to play baseball." Elway finished second to Herschel Walker for the 1983 Heisman Trophy. His baseball talents earned him a New York Yankees minor league contract, and gave Elway bargaining power when the Baltimore Colts picked him first overall in the 1983 draft. Baltimore traded its rights to Elway to Denver; there he became "The Duke of Denver" known for his NFL-record 41 fourth-quarter game-saving drives. His greatest moment may have come early in his career, on the road to Super Bowl XXI. He led the Broncos 98 yards in the final 5:32 of regulation to send the 1986 AFC title game into overtime. Denver beat the Cleveland Browns 23–20 in one of the most memorable games in NFL History. It became known as "The Drive."

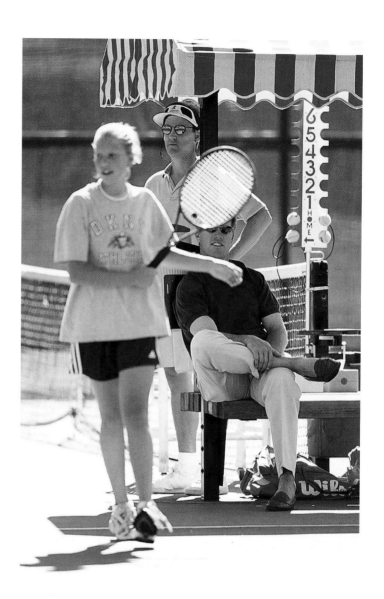

So untouched by age and experience . . .
They don't have the agendas . . .
They're pure, they are not tainted yet.

—JOHN

Afterword

Being an athlete is a great challenge, but being a father is an overwhelming job.

I work on my basketball game for hours each day to reduce the unpredictability of the outcome of the game. The more I practice my dribbling, shoot jump shots, and practice defensive schemes, the better chance I give myself to win games. The pressure to win is enormous, so I work on the mental aspect of the game. I focus on the successes, and visualize winning moments. There is a great deal of effort that is put into my career, because it is worth it. It is worth it when I shoot a sweet jumper and it dives through the net. It is worth it when we need a defensive stop and I'm able to come up with a big blocked shot. It is worth it when you stand on the platform at the end of the season crowned the NBA champions.

I have three children, all of them boys. I love to watch them grow up. Often, I take photos or videos of their progress. I love to teach them to read and write. I love to teach them Bible stories. We pray together and play together. In many ways fatherhood can be compared to being an athlete. You need to work hours each day on your job to reduce the possibility of failure. The pressure to raise good children is enormous, and in some ways, as a public figure, you face more than the normal challenges. But the reward is great, and it is worth it! As great as the excitement of winning is, it pales in comparison to the joy of fatherhood. If you experience success as a father, your legacy will not only be remembered, but it will multiply and reach far beyond your hopes and dreams.

—David Robinson

Photography Credits

Yogi Berra: AMY ROY (cover, 22, 23, 24, 25), Photo File, Inc. (25, action photo)

Terry Bradshaw: WILLIAM SNYDER (cover, xii, 1, 2, 3, 4, 5), Mike Fabus, Pittsburgh Steelers (5, action photo)

Roger Clemens: STEVE RAWLS (7), DIANE LONG (6, 8, 9), 1999, Rich Pilling/MLB Photos (8, action photo)

John Elway: WILLIAM SNYDER (154, 155, 156, 157, 158, 159), ©Ryan McKee/Rich Clarkson & Associates/NFL Photos (158, action photo)

Brett Favre: JUDY GRIESEDIECK (40, 41, 42, 43), Photo File, Inc. (41, action photo)

Doug Flutie: JOHN GOODMAN ©1999 (135), TONY O'BRIEN (134, 136, 137), John Grieshope/*Sports Illustrated* (137, action photo)

Gary Gait: SUSAN BIDDLE (52, 53), Russ Quackenbush (52, action photo)

Wayne Gretzky: WALTER IOOSS, JR. (138, 139, 140, 141, 142, 143), David Klutho/*Sports Illustrated* (138, action photo)

John Grisham: DEBORAH FEINGOLD (viii)

Dominic Hasek: JIM BUSH (66, 67), Damian Strohmeyer (67, action photo)

Orel Hershiser: BEN VAN HOOK (118, 119, 120, 121), 1999, Rich Pilling/MLB Photos (118, action photo)

Dan Jansen: MARK SLUDER (48, 49, 50, 51), John Biever/*Sports Illustrated* (48, action photo)

Tom Kite: STEVE RAWLS (54, 55, 56, 57), 2000 Stanbadz/PGA Tour (56, action photo)

Greg LeMond: JUDY GRIESEDIECK (90, 91), Graham Watson (91, action photo)

Howie Long: DIANE LONG (cover, 112, 113, 114, 115, 116, 117), Mickey Elliot (113, action photo)

Ronnie Lott: DEANNE FITZMAURICE (cover, 14, 15, 16, 17), Michael Zagaris (17, action photo)

Dan Marino: C.W. GRIFFIN (30, 31, 32, 33, 34, 35), Mitchell Reibel/NFL Photos (33, action photo)

Tino Martinez: BEN VAN HOOK (62, 63, 64, 65), 1999, Rich Pilling/MLB (64, action photo)

Tony Meola: AMY ROY (68, 69, 70, 71), Damian Strohmeyer/*Sports Illustrated* (68, action photo)

Joe Montana: WALTER IOOSS, JR. (144, 145, 146, 147), Michael Zagaris/NFL Photos (146, action photo)

Kyle Petty: MARK SLUDER (82, 83, 84, 85), Kevin Kane (82, action photo)

Richard Petty: MARK SLUDER (cover, 78, 79, 80, 81), Courtesy of Petty Enterprises (81, action photo)

Terry Porter: KEVIN GEIL (58, 59, 60, 61), Andy Hayt/NBA Photos (61, action photo)

David Robinson: CHARLIE CYR (161, action photo)

Ivan "Pudge" Rodriguez: AMY ROY (cover, 36, 37, 38, 39), Photo File, Inc. (39, action photo)

Junior Seau: DEANNE FITZMAURICE (cover, ii, 72, 73, 74, 75, 76, 77), Michael Nowak (77, action photo);

Shane Sellers: BILL LUSTER (130, 131, 132, 133), *Louisville Courier Journal* (131, action photo);

Sinjin Smith: GARY FRIEDMAN (26, 27, 28, 29), Leanne Robinson (28, action photo)

John Starks: DEANNE FITZMAURICE (126, 127, 128, 129), Sam Foreneich/NBA Photos (127, action photo)

Scott Stevens: AMY ROY (44, 45, 46, 47), Bruce Bennett (47, action photo)

Isiah Thomas: ALLAN LESSIG (18, 19, 20, 21), Andrew D. Bernstein/NBA Photos (18, action photo)

Scott Tinley: GARY FRIEDMAN (98, 99, 100, 101), Courtesy of Scott Tinley (99, action photo)

Keith Van Horn: AMY ROY (108, 109, 110, 111), Glen James/NBA Photos (110, action photo)

Governor Jesse Ventura: BILL LUSTER (10, 11, 12, 13), Walter Iooss, Jr./*Sports Illustrated* (11, action photo)

Peter Vermes: WILLIAM SNYDER (148, 149, 150, 151, 152, 153), Alan Yamamoto (149, action photo)

Peter Vidmar: GARY FRIEDMAN (122, 123, 124, 125), Norm Schindler/Terry O'Donnell/courtesy of UCLA (122, action photo)

Bill Walton: DEANNE FITZMAURICE (cover, 92, 93, 94, 95, 96, 97), Bill Baptist/NBA Photos (94, action photo)

Michael Weiss: SUSAN BIDDLE (86, 87, 88, 89), Kathy Goedeken (89, action photo)

Reggie White: SCOTT GOLDSMITH (cover, 102, 103, 104, 105, 106, 107), Steven Murphy/NFL Photos (103, action photo)

Acknowledgments

First, I thank the *He's Just My Dad!* fathers and children. They have given us all a personal gift, sharing their feelings, emotions, reflections, themselves.

I thank all the *He's Just My Dad!* moms. These women were essential in the creation of this project. There is no denying their huge influence on and importance to the families who shared themselves for the book. Many times the children being photographed would ask, "Why can't Mom be in the pictures?"

I thank my two teammates in this project, Merry and Frank Thomasson, for helping me take the first step and supporting me all the way to the finish line. Their blend of enthusiasm, energy, expertise, and levelheaded feedback and advice were the wings of the project.

I thank Sam Abell for sharing his outstanding experience, professionalism, and grace. I thank every member of our incredible team of photographers who artfully captured the unique spirit of each family.

I thank Jim Gibson and the staff at Gibson Design Associates for designing the book and making it all work.

I thank John Grisham for sharing his love of fatherhood and sports and his exceptional talent.

I thank David Robinson for contributing his thoughtful afterword.

I thank Elliott Kalb for his colorful biographies; Karen Whitehill, our editor, for her hard work under the gun; and Nancy Foley for her photo research.

I thank the Ford Motor Company and Value America for their generous support of *He's Just My Dad!*

I thank Anthea Disney and Jane Friedman of HarperCollins for their vision.

I thank the many athletes' representatives and assistants and our contacts in the league offices and team public relations departments for their support of this project.

I thank Bob Costas, David Hill, Mary Murray, Steve Rosner, Jeff Moorad, David Cornwell, Steve Horn, Dave Houghton, Mike Ornstein, Lucy Hood, Diane Barber, Bob Rotella, Christie Kite, Bob Capone, Anthony Delfre, Carolyn Achenbach, Shane Thomas and ALC Copies, Stubblefield Photo Lab, and Jeff Haas for their efforts and assistance.

I thank Chris Holden for being a loyal friend of the project from the very beginning.

I thank Amy Roy, whose relentless efforts kept making the project better and better. I thank my wonderful friends for their helpful suggestions and support.

I thank Betty Peters for sharing her incredible energy, contagious enthusiasm, and great pep talks. I could always count on Betty to get things done. She is a true friend.

I thank James Burke for his knowledgeable input and for keeping my roses alive.

Finally, I thank my husband, Howie, and our three sons Chris, Kyle, and Howie, for their priceless input, endless curiosity, and continuous love.